The New Answers Book 1

STUDY GUIDE & WORKBOOK

1:1
Answers IN GENESIS™

For more information, write:
Answers in Genesis, PO Box 510, Hebron, KY 41048

Printed in China

AnswersInGenesis.org

Contents

1

Is There Really a God?

1. How does design point to an Intelligent Creator God?

2. Both evolutionists and creationists agree that natural selection and mutations bring about change in an organism, but how do natural selection and mutations fall short in explaining design?

3. How does genetic information point to a Creator?

4. Why is a belief in God actually foundational to logical thought and scientific inquiry?

5. What is faith? What is the difference between faith in God and faith in evolution?

6. What is a difficulty some people have in accepting a Creator God?

2

Why Shouldn't Christians Accept Millions of Years?

1. List six reasons why a six-day creation is vital to the Christian faith.

2. How did the idea of millions of years come about? Who developed this idea?

3. Discuss the evidences of a young earth listed in the chapter, and discuss why each is significant.

3

Couldn't God Have Used Evolution?

1. How does the belief that God used evolution as His method of creation harm the gospel?

2. How does the belief that God used evolution as His method of creation harm the character of God?

3. The real issue behind saying that God used millions of years of evolution as His method of creation is that it puts the authority of God's Word against man's fallible opinion. How is this true?

4

Don't Creationists Deny the Laws of Nature?

1. How do these laws of nature confirm the Bible's testimony and/or contradict evolutionary teaching?
   a. Law of biogenesis

   b. Laws of chemistry

   c. Laws of planetary motion

   d. Laws of physics

e. Universal constants

f. The anthropic principle

g. Laws of mathematics

h. Laws of logic

i. Uniformity of nature

2. How are the laws of nature illogical within an atheistic worldview?

5

What About the Gap & Ruin-Reconstruction Theories?

1. In general, what is the gap theory?

2. Specifically, what is the "ruin-reconstruction" version of the gap theory?

3. How is the gap theory different from and similar to the ideas of "theistic evolution" and "progressive creation"?

4. Borrow copies of the *Scofield Reference Bible, Dake's Annotated Reference Bible,* and *The Newberry Reference Bible* from your local pastor or university library. Research for yourself what these books say concerning the gap theory.

5. What is the main reason people adhere to positions such as the gap theory?

6. Research Western Bible commentaries, written before the 18th century. How did the writers of these commentaries view Genesis 1–11 as a whole, and Genesis 1:1–2 in particular?

7. How does the message of the gap theory undermine the message of the gospel?

8. List and describe three biblical reasons that the gap theory cannot be true.

9. List and describe three non-biblical ways in which the gap theory is inconsistent.

10. How are the words *bara* and *asah* used in the Old Testament? Why should these words be considered interchangeable?

11. How does the actual grammatical structure of Genesis 1:1–2 preclude a gap of time being inserted?

12. Why is it inappropriate to translate the Hebrew word *hayetah* as “became” in the context of Genesis 1:1–2?

13. How do those who accept the gap theory translate *tohu* and *bohu*? Why do they translate them this way? What is the proper translation of these two words? Why?

14. How has the modern meaning of the word *replenish* been used to support the gap theory? Why is this inaccurate?

6

Cain's Wife—Who Was She?

1. Why is it important that Adam was the only man in the beginning?

2. Why is Jesus called the "Last Adam"?

3. Who was Cain's wife?

4. When was the Jewish law against intermarriage implemented? Why was it implemented?

7

Doesn't Carbon-14 Dating Disprove the Bible?

1. The carbon-dating method works on what types of substances?

2. Theoretically, how does carbon-dating work?

3. What is the critical assumption used in carbon-14 dating?

4. How would rejecting this assumption affect the outcome of one's experiments?

5. How could the global Flood have affected carbon-14 dating?

6. What findings did the recent RATE group record? How did they reach their conclusions?

7. What does carbon-14 dating prove about the age of the earth?

8

Could God Really Have Created Everything in Six Days?

1. What is the main reason some people believe Genesis 1 speaks of long ages?

2. Why is it inappropriate to refer to "nature" as the "67th book of the Bible"?

3. Why is it improper and unwise to use the findings of secular "origins" science to reinterpret Scripture?

4. Look up the word *day* in a Hebrew lexicon. Which Hebrew word refers to normal-length (approximately 24-hour) days? Long periods of time?

5. Which Hebrew word for *day* is used in Genesis 1?

6. Why is it important to consider the context when determining the meaning of a word?

7. Discuss and explain the eight objections to a literal, six-day creation and the answers to those objections.

8. How does the evolutionary order differ from the biblical order of creation?

9. What is theistic evolution? List some theological and scientific problems with accepting this view.

10. What is progressive creation? List some theological and scientific problems with accepting this view.

11. Why is important to accept that the days mentioned in Genesis 1 are regular-length days?

9

Does Radiometric Dating Prove the Earth Is Old?

1. Theoretically, how does radioisotope dating work?

2. What types of rocks are used with radioisotope dating?

3. Define half-life.

4. What critical assumptions are made in radioisotope dating?

5. How would rejecting these assumptions change the outcome of one's experiments?

6. Theoretically, how does isochron dating work?

7. How did the experiments done by the RATE group give evidence for a young earth?

10

Was There Really a Noah's Ark & Flood?

1. How was Noah able to build such a large, seaworthy vessel?

2. According to the Bible, what kinds of animals did Noah have with him on the Ark? What kinds of organisms were not on the Ark?

3. How is a "created kind" defined? How many "kinds" of animals were necessary for Noah to take on the Ark?

4. How did Noah care for all the animals on the Ark?

5. For the more technically minded: How seaworthy was the Ark?

6. According to the Bible, what were the two main sources of water for the global Flood of Noah's day?

7. Discuss the scriptural passages that show Noah's Flood was global.

8. Discuss the geological evidences that support a global Flood of Noah's day.

11

How Did Animals Spread All Over the World from Where the Ark Landed?

1. According to the Bible, how did all the animals get to the Ark?

2. Why do we not find fossils of kangaroos along the way from the Ark to Australia?

3. How did the Ice Age affect post-Flood animal and human distribution over the earth?

4. Explain the claims of the Recolonization Theory, and discuss the errors of this theory.

12
What Really Happened to the Dinosaurs?

1. In your own words, explain the history of dinosaurs according to evolutionists and according to the Bible.

2. Review the difference between *origins* science and *operational* science. Which aspects of paleontology fall under the realm of origins science? Which aspects are considered operational science?

3. Does the Bible mention dinosaurs? Where?

4. Discuss some evidences that show that dinosaur bones have not been around for millions of years.

5. Why is it important that we are able to explain the existence of dinosaurs within a biblical worldview?

13

Why Don't We Find Human & Dinosaur Fossils Together?

1. When asking the question of why we don't find human and dinosaur fossils together, what other factors should be taken into account? Why are these factors significant?

2. Does the lack of human fossils buried with dinosaur fossils support the evolutionary idea that humans and dinosaurs did not live together? Why or why not?

14

Can Catastrophic Plate Tectonics Explain Flood Geology?

1. In your own words, define *plate tectonics.*

2. What are the three types of horizontal movements of the earth's plates? What causes these movements?

3. Research the history of plate tectonics—how has it developed over the years?

4. How does observable evidence point to catastrophic movements of the earth's plates and not to slow-and-gradual movements?

5. What does the Bible say about catastrophic plate tectonics?

15

Don't Creationists Believe Some "Wacky" Things?

1. What "wacky" things have you, as a Christian, been accused of? How would you answer your accuser?

16

Where Does the Ice Age Fit?

1. How would the global Flood of Noah's day have provided the proper conditions for the Ice Age?

2. What evidences are there that support an Ice Age?

3. Give a brief explanation of an evolutionist's views about ice ages.

4. How do we know the Ice Age occurred *after* the Flood?

5. How long did the Ice Age last?

6. List the possible biblical references to the Ice Age.

7. Discuss the answer to the question, "What happened to the woolly mammoths?"

8. How does the Lake Missoula flood help us understand the impact of the global Flood?

17

Are There Really Different Races?

1. How have evolutionary-based ideas provided support for racism?

2. Explain, in your own words, how the characteristics of various people groups have come about.

3. What is the biblical basis and purpose for marriage?

4. Read Genesis 9:18–27. Who received the curse pronounced by Noah? Why did Noah pronounce this curse? Is the black "race" the result of a curse on Ham? Explain your answer.

5. List some biblical examples of so-called "interracial marriages" and explain the significance of them.

6. What is the only kind of "interracial" marriage the Bible forbids?

18

Are ETs & UFOs Real?

1. How does the idea of extra-terrestrial life stem largely from a belief in evolution?

2. What theological problems arise for those who believe alien races exist?

3. What is the primary motivation behind searching for "life" elsewhere in the universe?

19

Does Distant Starlight Prove the Universe Is Old?

1. Discuss the implications of the idea that God created light "on its way" on Day 4 of creation.

2. Discuss the assumptions that are involved in the light travel-time arguments. How does each affect the final result?

3. In your own words, explain the difference between universal time and local time.

4. Why is God not bound by the laws of nature?

5. What is the light travel-time problem present in the big bang model?

6. What is inflation? Does this explanation satisfy the light travel-time problem of the big bang model? Why or why not?

7. Answer the question posed in the chapter title.

20

Did Jesus Say He Created in Six Literal Days?

1. List and discuss the Old Testament and New Testament passages of Scripture in which Jesus states the young age of the earth.

2. What Old Testament accounts does Jesus treat as historical fact? What impact do Jesus' claims have?

21

How Did Defense/Attack Structures Come About?

1. How does the idea that defense/attack structures were part of God's original design impact man's view of God and His character?

2. According to Genesis 3, is the world as we see it the same as it was in the beginning? If not, what changed the world?

3. List the passages of Scripture that address the changes in nature, and discuss each change.

4. What are the two primary alternatives that explain defense/attack structures from a biblical perspective?

5. Along with the Curse proclaimed in Genesis 3, what else did God promise? Why is this significant?

22

Is Natural Selection the Same Thing as Evolution?

1. What is the definition of *natural selection* from an evolutionist's perspective? From a creationist's perspective?

2. Who was one of the first to formulate the theory of natural selection? How was his theory different from Darwin's?

3. How did natural selection benefit animals in the post-Flood world?

4. Discuss the limitations of natural selection. How do these support biblical creation and not evolution?

5. Define *species*.

6. What has been observed about the formation of new species? How does this support a young earth?

23

Hasn't Evolution Been Proven True?

1. What is the significance of the differences between the creation order of events and the evolutionary order of events?

2. What is the problem with the cosmologists' claim that a vacuum can, under some circumstances, give rise to matter?

3. How did Miller's chemical experiment fail to fully produce life from non-life?

4. What is "comparative anatomy"? What do the differences between such structures prove about their Creator's purposes? What do the similarities prove about their Creator?

5. Did Darwin's observations about the differences in finch beaks on the Galapagos Islands help him prove his theory, or did they disprove his theory?

24

Did Dinosaurs Turn into Birds?

1. What are the differences between what the Bible says and what evolutionists claim about the origin of birds and the origin of dinosaurs?

2. What are the differences between the blood, hips, "hands," and lungs of birds and those of dinosaurs?

3. What fossil was touted by biology textbooks as the perfect transitional fossil? What has been proven about this fossil?

25

Does Archaeology Support the Bible?

1. What is the special role of the Bible, regarding its relation between God and man?

2. Discuss the archaeological evidences that support the Bible's accuracy in Genesis 1–11.

3. Discuss the archaeological evidences that support the Bible's accuracy in Genesis 11–36.

4. Discuss the archaeological evidences that support the Bible's accuracy in Genesis 37–50.

5. Discuss the archaeological evidences that support the Bible's accuracy in Exodus to Deuteronomy.

6. Discuss the archaeological evidences that support the Bible's accuracy in dealing with the time of Joshua through the time of Saul.

7. Discuss the archaeological evidences that support the Bible's accuracy in dealing with the time of David through the time of Solomon.

8. Discuss the archaeological evidences that support the Bible's accuracy in dealing with the Assyrian Period.

9. Discuss the archaeological evidences that support the Bible's accuracy in dealing with the Babylonians and Nebuchadnezzar.

10. Discuss the archaeological evidences that support the Bible's accuracy in dealing with Cyrus and the Medes and Persians.

11. Discuss the archaeological evidences that support the Bible's accuracy in dealing with Ezra and Nehemiah.

12. Discuss the archaeological evidences that support the Bible's accuracy in dealing with the information in the Dead Sea Scrolls.

13. Discuss the archaeological evidences that support the Bible's accuracy in dealing with the Person of our Lord.

14. Discuss the archaeological evidences that support the Bible's accuracy in dealing with the New Testament, the early church, and the early years of Christianity.

15. Why is the study of archaeology beneficial to Christians?

16. Discuss and memorize the acrostic that shows archaeology's relevance to the Bible.

26

Why Does God's Creation Include Death & Suffering?

1. In a Hebrew dictionary, look up the term *nephesh* and write its definitions. How is the word used in Genesis 1?

2. What kinds of things have *nephesh* life?

3. Why did God's command to Adam and the animals to eat plants for food *not* involve death, in the biblical sense?

4. Why is there so much death and suffering in the world today?

5. How did sin impact the earth and mankind in the past? Today?

6. How does having an evolutionary foundation impact one's views on death and suffering? How does it impact man's hope for the future?

7. What hope is there for Christians who are struggling through physical trials?

27

How Can I Use This Information to Witness?

1. Describe someone who is typed as a "Jew" (according to the context of this chapter).

2. Describe someone who is typed as a "Greek" (according to the context of this chapter).

3. What did the Jews, who lived around the time of Jesus, already understand about creation, the Fall, sin, the law of Moses, and sacrifices?

4. How did Peter address these Jews in light of what they understood?

5. What did the Greeks who lived around the time of Jesus *not* understand about creation, the Fall, sin, the law of Moses, and sacrifices?

6. How did Paul address them in light of what they understood?

7. How have most modern nations of today changed from being like the Jews of old to the Greeks of old?

8. What is vital to a Christian's evangelism in today's Greek culture?

9. How can *you* use the information you have gained from this book?